Punctuation Plus Comprehensi

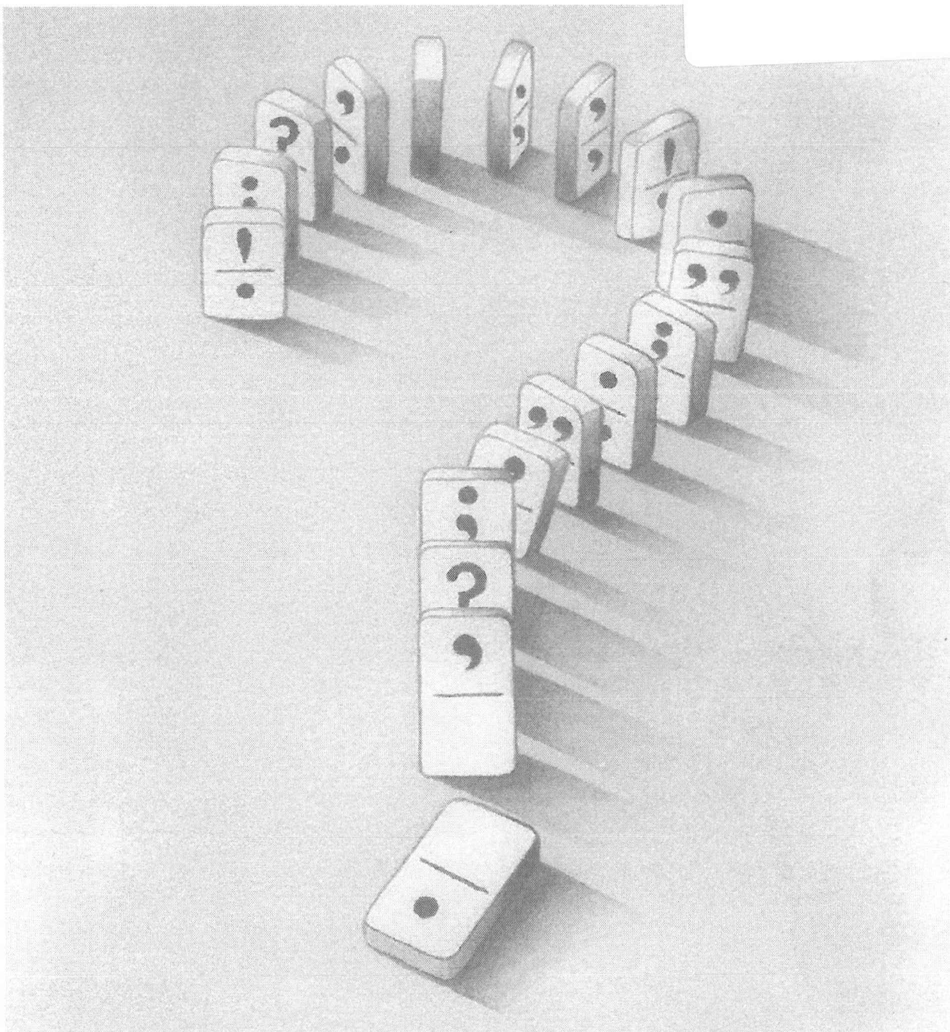

Diane Butterfield

Egon Publishers Ltd
618 Leeds Road, Outwood
Wakefield WF1 2LT
www.egon.co.uk

Punctuation Plus Comprehension

ISBN: 978-1873533 91 8
First published: 2002
Reprinted and revised: 2017

Egon Publishers Ltd
618 Leeds Road, Outwood
Wakefield WF1 2LT
Tel/FAX: 01924 871697
www.egon.co.uk
information@egon.co.uk

For more books on Punctuation and Comprehension:

978-1873533 59 8	Practise Punctuation – Book 0
978-1873533 28 4	Practise Punctuation – Book 1
978-1873533 29 1	Practise Punctuation – Book 2

978-1873533 92 5	Practise Comprehension – Book 0
978-1873533 96 3	Practise Comprehension – Book 1
978-1873533 95 6	Practise Comprehension – Book 2

Punctuation Plus Comprehension

Contents

Punctuation Plus Comprehension

About this book

This book can be used in conjunction with Practise Punctuation - Book 0.

It is split into stages covering capital letters, sentences, question marks and exclamation marks. Simple texts are used to cover each of the areas. Several sentences are grouped together in order for pupils to have plenty of practise in recognising sentences and to boost their comprehension skills. This improves awareness of correct sentence construction and use of capital letters and full stops.

How to use this book

Read out the instructions to the pupils. All the pages can be differentiated by omitting parts of the task when photocopying as some of the comprehension tasks maybe too difficult for the lower ability pupils.

Pupils should be encouraged to read their work aloud. This will help them to understand the connection between the pauses, emphasis and intonation in the spoken words and the punctuation marks of the written sentences.

Hilda King.

Name_ _ _ _ _ _ _ _ _ _ _ _ _ _ _ _ _ _ Date _ _ _ _ _ _ _ _ _

Capital letters

Add the capital letters.

The first one is done for you.

Try to do it faster then your partner.

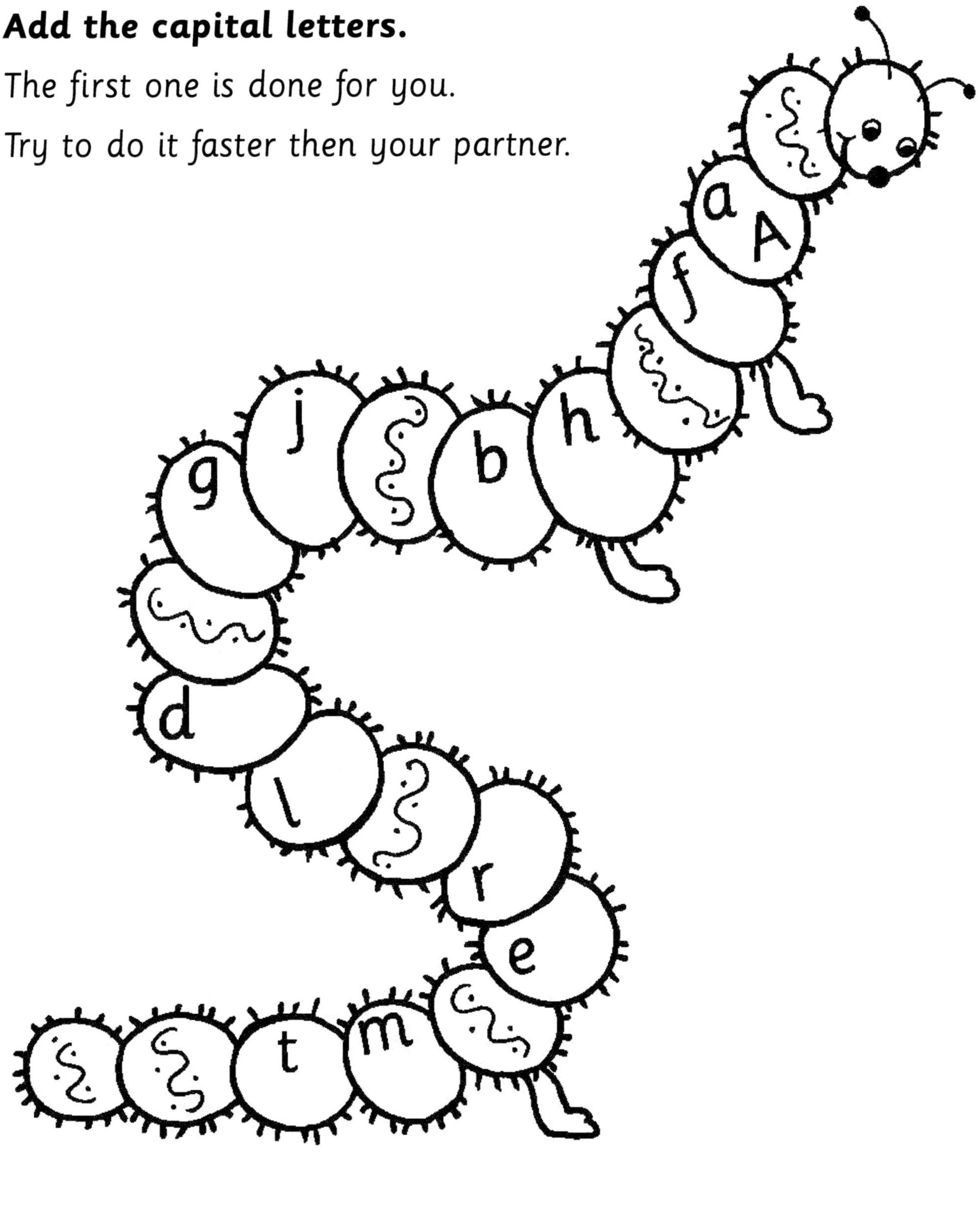

Name________________ Date _________

Capital letters and full stops

A sentence is a group of words that make sense. Each sentence starts with a capital letter and ends with a full stop.

Underline the sentences.

1. The ant ran on the log.
2. Sam likes his
3. Tom has a red ball.
4. Dad is in his big van.
5. The pond was full of
6. A boy big

Make these words into sentences.

1. The cat went ____________________
2. My Mum ____________________
3. I like to ____________________
4. Sam has a ____________________
5. I can kick a ____________________
6. The dogs bark at the ____________________

Write a sentence of your own about your family.

____

____

Name_ _ _ _ _ _ _ _ _ _ _ _ _ _ _ _ _ Date _ _ _ _ _ _ _ _ _

Writing sentences

Read the words on the leaves.

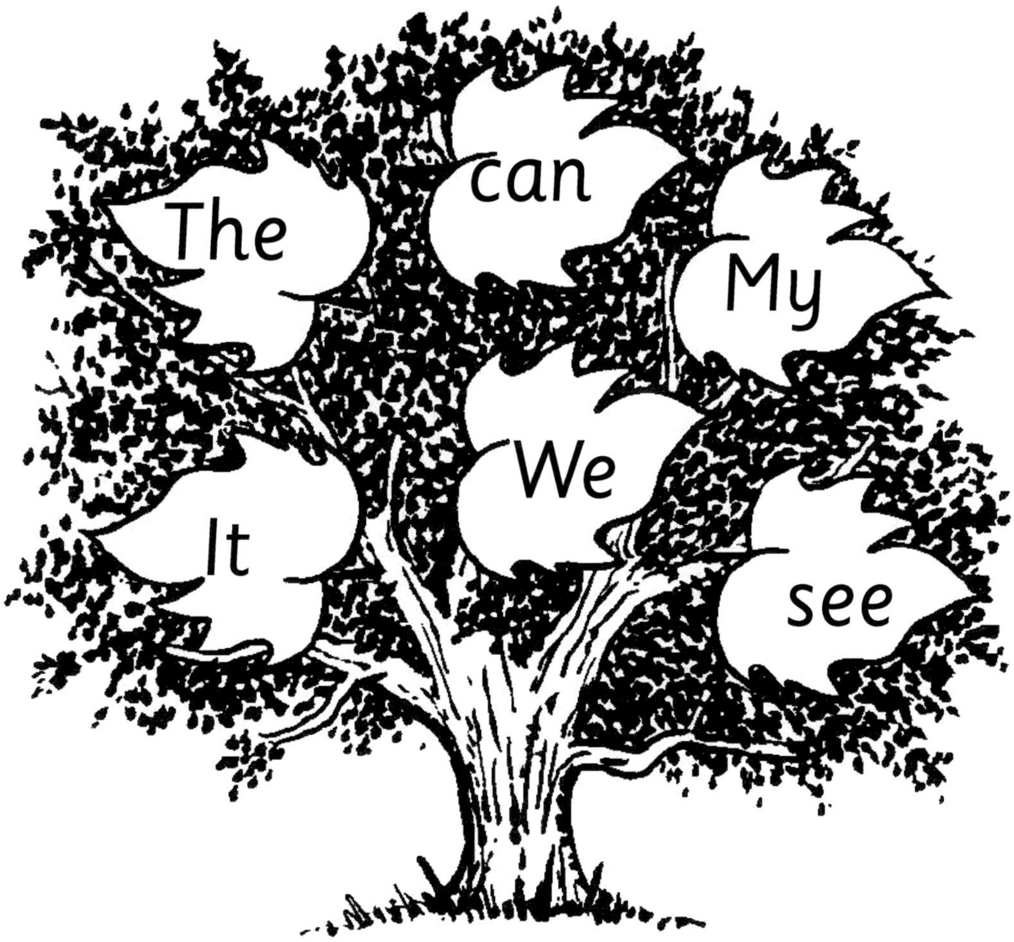

Colour those that start with a capital letter.

Write a sentence with the words that begin with a capital letter.

1. ______________________________

2. ______________________________

3. ______________________________

4. ______________________________

Name_ _ _ _ _ _ _ _ _ _ _ _ _ _ _ _ Date _ _ _ _ _ _ _ _

Writing sentences

Capital letters are not found in the middle of words.

Read the sentences below.

What is wrong with them?

Write the sentence on the lines below as they should be written. The first one is done for you.

1. I sAw the Fox in the woOD.

   I saw the fox in the wood.

2. Mum is iN the batH.

3. The PiG is in hIs sTy.

4. Sam FeLL oFF the waLl.

5. I have a Big Doll.

6. We aRe in thE Park.

7. The Cat is IN itS Box.

Name_ _ _ _ _ _ _ _ _ _ _ _ _ _ _ _ _ Date _ _ _ _ _ _ _ _ _

Writing sentences

The sun is hot. Sam is on the sand. He can see a red crab.

Read the sentences above.

How many are there? ____________________

Underline each sentence in a different colour.

Add something to the picture and colour it.

Write one or more sentences below.

1. ____

2. ____

3. ____

Take turns to read your sentences with a partner.

Name_ _ _ _ _ _ _ _ _ _ _ _ _ _ _ _ Date _ _ _ _ _ _ _ _ _

Writing sentences

Spot is a big dog. Sam and Ben like to play with a ball. Spot ran off with their ball. Sam was cross. Can they get him to come back?

Read the sentences above.

How many sentences are there? ____________

Underline each sentence in a different colour.

Draw the dog in the picture and colour it.

What happened to the ball?

____

Finish the story and say how you think Sam got Spot back.

____

____

____

Take turns to read your sentences with a partner.

Name_ _ _ _ _ _ _ _ _ _ _ _ _ _ _ _ _ Date _ _ _ _ _ _ _ _ _

Writing sentences

It is Sam's birthday. Sam and his Mum are going to the shops. They look in the toy shop for ideas. Sam says that he would like a toy car for his birthday. He picks a red one. Sam goes to play with his friend Ben. They push their cars down the garden path. The cars fall into some mud. Sam's new car is very dirty.

Read the sentences above.

How many sentences are there? ______________________

Underline the first word of each sentence.

What do you notice? ______________________

What do you think happened next? Was Mum cross? Was Sam upset?

Write one or more sentences below.

____

____

____

____

Take turns to read your sentences with a partner.

Name_ _ _ _ _ _ _ _ _ _ _ _ _ _ _ _ _ _ Date _ _ _ _ _ _ _ _ _

Punctuating sentences

Add capital letters and full stops to each sentence.

There are two sentences in each line.

Write them out correctly on the lines.

1. sam has a bat he can hit a ball with it

2. ben is by the pond a fish is in his net

3. tom fell on the path he cut his leg

4. the cat sat in the sun it was a hot day

5. it was mum's birthday she had a party

6. the dog was wet he went to lie down in his box

Write two sentences about a dog, or any animal.

Name_ _ _ _ _ _ _ _ _ _ _ _ _ _ _ _ _ Date _ _ _ _ _ _ _ _ _

Capital letters for names

Look at the four pictures. In each box write the name of someone in your class. Remember people's names always begin with a capital letter. **In the middle box draw a picture of your teacher and add her or his name.**

Write one or two sentences about your friends.

Name_ _ _ _ _ _ _ _ _ _ _ _ _ _ _ _ _ Date _ _ _ _ _ _ _ _ _

Punctuating sentences

Add capital letters and full stops to each sentence.

There are three sentences in each part.

sam and his class are going on a school trip they are going on a bus miss moss is taking them to a farm

they got to the farm at ten ‘clock sam saw a brown cow in a field it was eating grass

miss moss went to see the farmer he showed them some fat pigs they were sitting in the mud

the class looked at some ducks they were on the farmer’s pond five ducklings were with them

Do you think that the farm is in the country?

Give two reasons for your answer.

Name________________ Date ________

Punctuating sentences

Sam went to the pet shop with Mum he saw a big brown dog the cats were playing with a ball there were three red and three yellow fish in a tank a hamster was running in her wheel

There are five sentences above.

Underline each in a different colour, then read them to your partner.

Add in the full stops and capital letters.

Colour the picture and add a ball and some fish to it.

Finish the story by writing more sentences below.

Name_ _ _ _ _ _ _ _ _ _ _ _ _ _ _ _ Date _ _ _ _ _ _ _ _ _

Punctuating sentences

Sam was on holiday with his family they had gone to Scotland on Sunday they all went to see a castle the castle was on a hill dad paid for them to go inside it was dark and gloomy they went down into the dungeon Sam fell over he had tripped on an old box.

There are nine sentences in the passage above.
Add in the full stops and capital letters.
Read the story to your partner. Does it make sense?

Do you think that the castle was on high ground?
Give your reason.

Where do you think the dungeon was?

Name_ _ _ _ _ _ _ _ _ _ _ _ _ _ _ _ Date _ _ _ _ _ _ _ _ _

Free writing

Draw your family in the box, then write about your family and pets.
Underline each name in coloured pencil.
Have you used a captial letter for each name?

My name is....

Name________________ Date _________

Free writing

Read the story.

__________ likes to play football with __________

and __________. They play in the local park.

__________ kicked the ball to __________.

He missed it. The ball fell into the duck pond.

Mr __________ came to help retrieve it.

How many children are there? ________

Give each one a name of your choice.

Don't forget to start each name with a capital letter.

Who came to help? Give him a name.

Finish the story by saying what happened next.

____

____

____

Name_ _ _ _ _ _ _ _ _ _ _ _ _ _ _ _ _ Date _ _ _ _ _ _ _ _ _

Days of the week

Days of the week have capital letters.

Monday **T**uesday **W**ednesday **T**hursday

Friday **S**aturday **S**unday

Write a sentence in the diary for each day of the week.

Draw a picture in the spaces in the diary.

Monday I went to see Gran.	
T________ I made buns with Mum.	
________ I took my dog for a walk.	
________	
________	
________	
________	

Name________________ Date ________

Days of the week

Read the story below.

Put in the capital letters for the days of the week.

Last August Sam went on holiday to Spain. On day he swam in the pool. It was very hot so they all went to the sandy beach on day. The rain fell all day on day but it was not cold. On lay they had a ride in a boat.

Write your own sentences for the rest of Sam's week.

Write out the days of the week on a seperate sheet of paper, try not to look back at the list given.

Name________________ Date _________

Months of the year

Months of the year start with capital letters.

January	**J**uly
February	**S**eptember
March	**O**ctober
April	**N**ovember
May	**D**ecember

Answer the questions below with the correct month.

1. We put up the Christmas tree in ____________.
2. A new year starts in ____________.
3. We start a new school year in ____________.
4. The leaves fall from the trees in ____________.
5. We don't go to school in ____________.

Write a sentence each about your birthday, your holiday, your Mum's birthday and Bonfire night.

____

____

____

____

____

____

Name_ _ _ _ _ _ _ _ _ _ _ _ _ _ _ _ Date _ _ _ _ _ _ _ _ _

Months of the year

Put in the capital letters for the months of the year.

In ___eptember Sam went into Class Three. In ___ctober he took some carrots from his Dad's allotment to the harvest assembly. Sam fell down and cut his leg in ___ovember. He was a sheep in the nativity play in ___ecember. It was cold and the snow fell at playtime in ___anuary.
On 17th ___ebruary it was his birthday. All the class went in a red bus to the zoo in ___arch.

Write your own sentences for the rest of the year.

In ___pril ______________________________

____

____

____

Draw a picture in the box showing a month of the year.

The picture shows the month of ______________.

Name_ _ _ _ _ _ _ _ _ _ _ _ _ _ _ _ Date _ _ _ _ _ _ _ _ _

Place names

Draw your house in the box.

Remember: places have capital letters.

Write your address underneath.

____

____

____

____

Fill in the spaces below with the name of a place:

1. The Queen lives in ____________ ____________.
2. I went on holiday to ____________.
3. My Auntie Jess lives in ____________.
4. My school is in ____________.
5. London is the capital city of ____________.

Name_ _ _ _ _ _ _ _ _ _ _ _ _ _ _ _ _ Date _ _ _ _ _ _ _ _ _

Place names

Find the place names and underline them, then add the capital letters.

Sam went to stay in london with his friend Ben. Ben lived in green lane. Ben's Uncle Jim had come to stay with them from america. They all went to see buckingham palace and the tower of london. On Sunday they had a picnic by the river thames and went for a walk in hyde park.

Where you would take Sam if he came to visit you? Write about at least three places.

Name________________ Date _________

Revision and comprehension

Find and underline the words that should have capital letters.

it was a hot sunday in june. Sam and his family went to blackpool for the day. Auntie sue and uncle chris went too. The family sat in greenwood park and had a picnic. Six hungry ducks came up from the pond. His mum fed them with bread. One greedy duck snatched a bun out of Sam's hand. He was cross.

Do you think that it was raining? Give two reasons.

____

____

____

Why was Sam cross when the duck took his bun?

____

____

Name________________ Date ________

Question marks

Trace over the question marks, then practice your own.

? ? ? ? ? ______________

Add a question mark or a full stop to the sentences below to make them correct.

1. How are you
2 The girls are singing in the hall
3. I like chocolate
4. When is your birthday
5 Do you like apples
6. I can skip
7. Can we go to the shops
8. Is your cat ill

Write a question to go with each statement (answer). Don't forget to add a question mark at the end of your question.

1. ______________________ I am in the bathroom.
2. ______________________ The time is 5 o'clock.
3. ______________________ Let's play cards.
4. ______________________ I like fish and chips.
5. ______________________ I am happy.
6. ______________________ We can run fast.
7. ______________________ I am cold.
8. ______________________ We like school.

Name_ _ _ _ _ _ _ _ _ _ _ _ _ _ _ _ Date _ _ _ _ _ _ _ _ _

Question marks

Sam and Ben went to the woods. Spot the dog was with them. Spot ran away. "Where are you " said Sam. "Is he in the bushes " asked Ben. They could not find him anywhere. "Do you think that he is having a game with us Do you think that he ran away so that we would play with him " asked Sam.

How many sentences are there? ______________

How many questions are there? ______________

Underline the questions and add question marks.

Draw Spot peeping around the tree.

Finish the story.

Name_ _ _ _ _ _ _ _ _ _ _ _ _ _ _ _ _ Date _ _ _ _ _ _ _ _ _

Exclamation marks

Trace the exclamation marks and practice writing them.

! ! ! ! ! ______________

Rewrite these sentences, putting in the exclamation marks:

1. "Wait I have lost my shoe."

____

2 "Hooray " said Sam. "We won the cup."

____

3. "What a lovely day " said Mum. "Let's go to the seaside."

____

4. "Don't do that " shouted Dad.

____

5 The man shouted, "Stop "

____

Write three sentences using these words:

Help Well done Oh dear

____

____

____

Name_ _ _ _ _ _ _ _ _ _ _ _ _ _ _ _ _ Date _ _ _ _ _ _ _ _ _

Question and exclamation marks

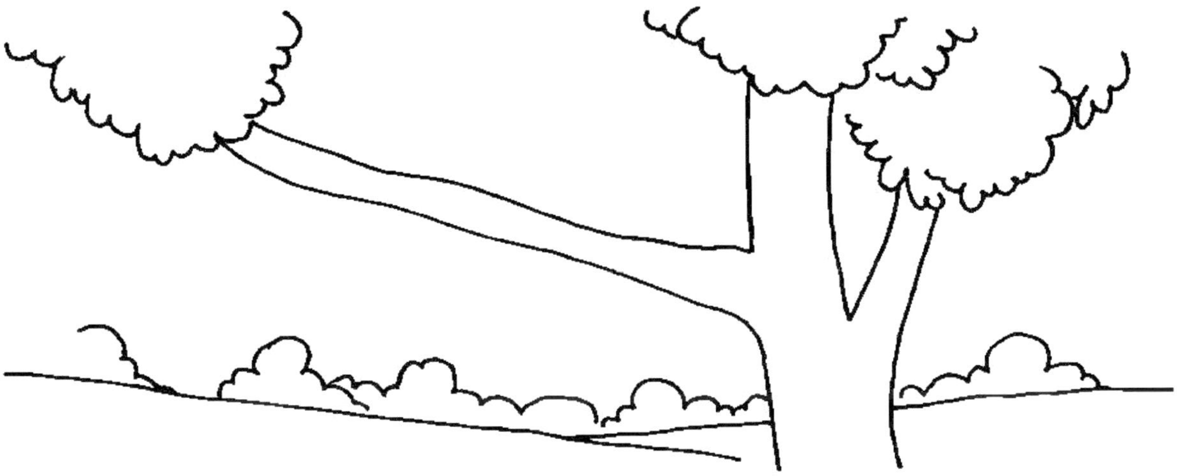

Put in the question marks and exclamation marks in the story below.

Sam has a black and white cat called Tess. One day she got stuck in a tree. "Oh, no " said Sam, "What shall I do " Sam went up the tree and sat on a branch, He put out his hand to grab Tess but she jumped down. "Help " shouted Sam, "I'm stuck. Can anyone hear me "

Do you think Sam was happy to be in the tree?
Give at least two reasons in your answer below.

____

____

____

____

Draw Tess in the tree.

Name_ _ _ _ _ _ _ _ _ _ _ _ _ _ _ _ _ Date _ _ _ _ _ _ _ _ _

Question and exclamation marks

Add the missing punctuation to the stories below.
Rewrite and finish each story.

sam had a new bike last saturday he rode down cross street to see ben “wow” shouted ben “may I have a go, please ”

Mum came into the room on her head was a new hat “do you like it” asked Mum. “you look lovely ” said dad “I shall wear it to tim’s wedding in july ” said mum.